SCHOLASTIC **discover more**™

See Me Grow

By Penelope Arlon
and Tory Gordon-Harris

How to discover more

See Me Grow is specially planned to help you discover more about animals and how they grow.

Big words and pictures introduce an important subject.

Picture sequences show what happens in detail.

Small words help you explore pictures for active reading.

Egg to chick

A hen lays eggs, as all birds do. She sits on the eggs to keep them warm until they hatch into chicks.

The chick uses a special egg tooth to break the shell.

The hen sits on her eggs to keep them warm and safe.

When a chick has grown too big for its shell, it hatches.

As it grows into a chicken, the chick's feathers change colour.

eggshell

A chick spends 21 days in the egg before it hatches.

16

17

The glossary explains words; the index helps you find them.

Digital companion book

Download your free all-new digital book, **See Me Grow Fun!**

Log on to
www.scholastic.com/ discovermore

Enter your unique code:
RM6DTMFN4T22

Fun animal activities

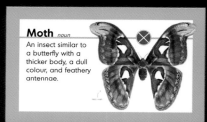

Moth *noun*
An insect similar to a butterfly with a thicker body, a dull colour, and feathery antennae.

More animal words

Contents

Copyright 2012 by Scholastic Inc.

All rights reserved. Published by Scholastic Inc., Publishers since 1920. SCHOLASTIC, SCHOLASTIC DISCOVER MORE™ and associated logos are trademarks and/or registered trademarks of Scholastic Inc.

No part of this publication may be reproduced, stored in a retrieval system, or transmitted in any form or by any means, electronic, mechanical, photocopying, recording, or otherwise, without the written permission of the publisher. For information regarding permission, please write to Scholastic Inc., Attention: Permissions Department, 557 Broadway, New York, NY 10012.

Distributed in the UK by
Scholastic UK Ltd
Westfield Road
Southam, Warwickshire
England CV47 0RA

Library of Congress Cataloging-in-Publication Data Available

ISBN 978 1407 13154 2

10 9 8 7 6 5 4 3 2 1   12 13 14 15 16

Printed in Singapore 46
First edition, March 2012 HB

Scholastic is constantly working to lessen the environmental impact of our manufacturing processes.
To view our industry-leading paper procurement policy, visit www.scholastic.com/paperpolicy.

Animal babies

Some animal babies hatch
from eggs laid by their mothers.
Other animal babies grow
inside their mothers' tummies.

Insects

Most insects lay eggs.
Some eggs are blue;
others are green
or yellow.

Fish

Most fish lay eggs.
They sometimes
lay hundreds of
eggs at one time.

Amphibians

Most amphibians
lay eggs.
They lay them
in water.

A butterfly is
an insect.

All fish live, and lay
their eggs, in water.

Frogs and toads are
amphibians.

Hatching eggs

Baby birds have to crack their eggs open and climb out.

baby ostrich inside an egg

Mammals

Most mammals don't lay eggs. Their babies grow inside the mothers' tummies.

Birds

Birds lay eggs. The parents sometimes sit on the eggs until they hatch.

Reptiles

Most reptiles lay eggs. Their eggs are sometimes soft.

Alligators are reptiles.

Birds often make nests for their eggs.

Rabbits

Baby rabbits are very little when they are born, but they grow up fast.

Baby rabbits are called kittens.

Rabbits are mammals.

A baby rabbit can have more than 10 brothers and sisters!

Baby rabbits are born pink and hairless. Their eyes are closed.

After a few days, soft baby fur grows and the kittens' eyes open.

At two weeks old, the kittens leave the nest and find their own food.

From caterpillar

Butterfly babies don't look like butterflies at all. Follow their journey.

From egg to adult

A butterfly lays a round egg.

A caterpillar hatches out of the egg.

The caterpillar eats and eats.

It covers itself with a cocoon for protection.

to butterfly

A butterfly is an insect.

Changes take place inside the cocoon.

After two weeks, the cocoon opens.

A butterfly climbs out of the cocoon.

The butterfly flies away.

9

A frog's life

Baby frogs live in water.
Grown-up frogs live on
land and in water.

From tadpole to frog

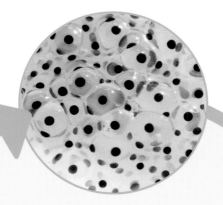

A mother frog lays her eggs, called frogspawn, in water.

The eggs hatch into tadpoles that swim in water.

frog

Frogs are amphibians. The tadpoles breathe in water, but the grown-ups breathe in air and water.

tadpoles

Soon the tadpoles turn into frogs. Grown-up frogs jump around on land and splash in water.

The tadpoles grow legs and slowly lose their tails.

In a pouch

A baby kangaroo is called a joey. It lives in its mother's pouch.

The mother's pouch is a pocket in her tummy.

kangaroo

joey

A joey sometimes sticks its head out of the pouch!

A new joey is tiny. It climbs straight into its mother's pouch.

The mother makes milk. The joey drinks it inside her pouch.

After about six months of growing the joey climbs out.

These mammals with pouches live in Australia.

koala

joey

After about six months, a baby koala leaves its mother's pouch and hitches a ride!

Shark babies

Many sharks lay eggs. Shark eggs can be unusual shapes and sizes.

Baby sharks are born with a lot of sharp teeth!

The dogfish shark lays eggs called mermaid's purses.

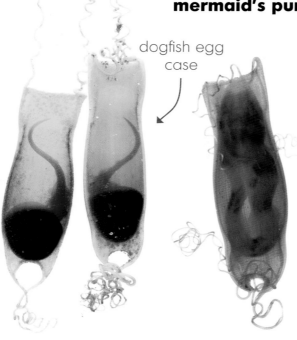

dogfish egg case

dogfish shark

The shark lays a pair of egg cases on the sea floor.

The baby sharks grow inside the cases.

When the sharks are ready, they break out.

The baby sharks have to survive alone in the sea.

Sharks are fish. Many sharks lay eggs. This great white shark has eggs that hatch inside her, so she gives birth to live young.

Leopard sharks give birth to up to 33 live babies at once.

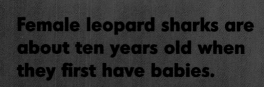

Female leopard sharks are about ten years old when they first have babies.

Egg to chick

A hen lays eggs, as all birds do. She sits on the eggs to keep them warm until they hatch into chicks.

The chick uses a special egg tooth to break the shell.

eggshell

The hen sits on her eggs to keep them warm and safe.

When a chick has grown too big for its shell, it hatches.

As it grows into a chicken, the chick grows new feathers.

A chick spends 21 days in the egg before it hatches.

Bee grubs

Honeybees live in big groups and look after their babies together.

Nectar is a sugary liquid made by some flowers.

Bees make nests out of wax. The queen bee lays one egg in each little cell.

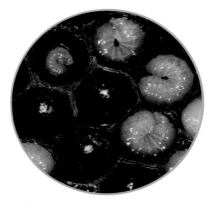

After three days, the eggs hatch into babies, called grubs.

At six days old, the grub wraps itself in a cocoon and changes inside it.

queen bee

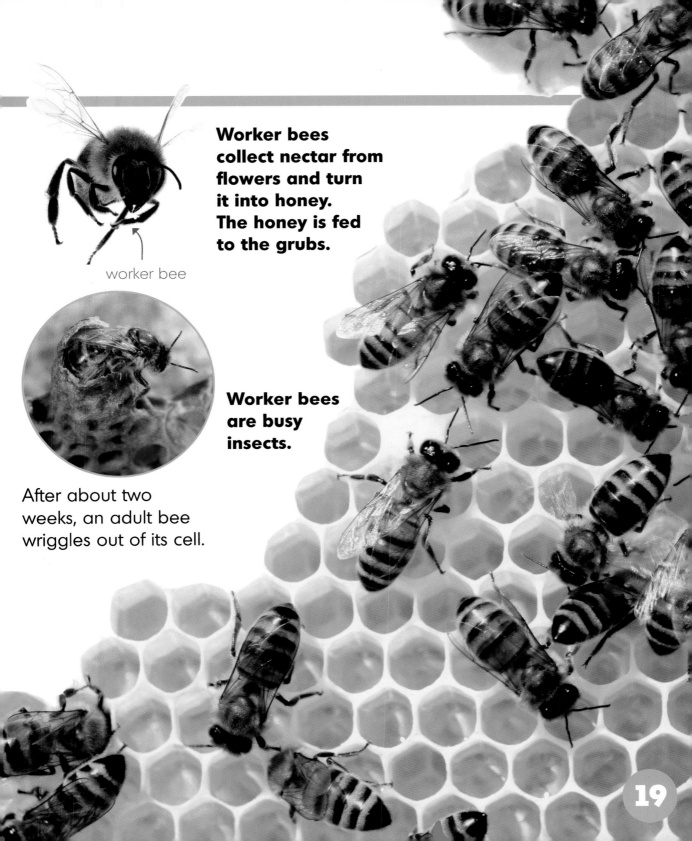

Worker bees collect nectar from flowers and turn it into honey. The honey is fed to the grubs.

worker bee

Worker bees are busy insects.

After about two weeks, an adult bee wriggles out of its cell.

Alligators

Alligators, like all reptiles, lay eggs that hatch into babies.

An alligator is born with a full set of sharp teeth.

The mother alligator sometimes carries her babies to the water in her mouth.

The female alligator makes a nest out of mud and plants. She lays 25 to 50 eggs.

The mother guards her eggs. After about two months, the babies hatch.

The mother takes the babies down to the water. The baby alligators can swim straight away.

Alligator babies stay with their mothers for up to two years.

baby alligator

Clownfish hide
in poisonous sea
anemones for safety.

Fish babies

Clownfish live among coral reefs. These fish lay hundreds of eggs on rocks.

clownfish babies

Clownfish lay their eggs close to poisonous sea anemones. Doing this helps keep the eggs safe from fish that like to eat them.

From eggs to young

eggs

Clownfish lay hundreds of eggs. The parents guard them fiercely.

About five days later, the eggs hatch into tiny clownfish.

The baby fish swim away and find food by themselves.

Baby horses

Baby horses can run when they are very young to escape danger in the wild.

A horse is a mammal.

A wild foal stays close to its mother for about a year.

Horse babies are called foals.

The foal grows inside its mother's tummy until it is ready to be born.

The foal can stand up and walk around minutes after being born.

The mother horse makes milk in her body for the foal to drink.

After a few days, the foal can gallop faster than you can.

Puppies

Dogs can have litters of up to 12 puppies, but most litters have about six.

Birth

A mother dog gives birth to a litter of puppies.

Female dogs, like all mammals, make milk inside their bodies. The puppies drink the milk for 2 months.

26

food for Mum!

1 day

The puppies can smell their mother's milk at 1 day old.

10 days

At about 10 days old, the puppies open their eyes.

4 weeks

At 4 weeks old, the puppies can wag their tails and bark.

2 months

By 2 months, the puppies no longer need their mother.

Puppies love to roll around and play, just as human children do.

American robins hatch from beautiful bright blue eggs.

Baby birds

Robins, like many birds, lay their eggs in nests they make in trees.

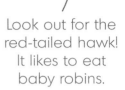

Look out for the red-tailed hawk! It likes to eat baby robins.

The mother makes a nest and lays her eggs.

The baby birds are born blind and without feathers.

The chicks open their mouths wide to be fed.

The parents feed the chicks insects and berries.

At two weeks, the chicks are ready to leave.

The chicks leap out of the nest and fly away.

29

Glossary

Amphibian
A cold-blooded animal. Most amphibians spend part of their lives in water and part of their lives on land. Frogs and toads are amphibians.

Bird
An animal with feathers, wings, and a beak. It is a warm-blooded animal.

Caterpillar
A young form of a butterfly or moth.

Chick
A young bird.

Cocoon
A case made by some baby insects to cover themselves. The cocoon protects the baby insect inside.

Coral reef
A ridge made of coral that lies in the sea. Coral is made of animal skeletons.

Fish
A cold-blooded animal that lives in water and has scales, fins, and gills.

Foal
A young horse.

Frogspawn
The eggs of a frog. Jelly surrounds the eggs.

Grub
A young insect, such as a bee.

Hen
An adult female bird, such as a chicken.

Insect
A small animal with a body that has three main parts. An insect has six legs and may have wings. Butterflies and bees are insects.

Kitten
A young cat or rabbit.

Litter
A group of baby animals that are born at one time from one mother.

Mammal
A warm-blooded animal. Mammals feed milk to their young and usually have hair. Dogs and humans are mammals.

Puppy
A young dog.

Reptile
A cold-blooded animal. Reptiles usually have scaly skin and lay eggs. Alligators and snakes are reptiles.

Sea anemone
An animal with a body shaped like a tube and a mouth that is surrounded by stinging tentacles.

Index

Thank you

Art Director: Bryn Walls
Designer: Ali Scrivens
Managing Editor: Miranda Smith
Editor: Slaney Begley
Cover Designer: Natalie Godwin
DTP: John Goldsmid
Picture Research: Dwayne Howard
**Executive Director of
Photography, Scholastic:** Steve Diamond

Photography credits
1: B. Stefanov/Shutterstock; 3t: Comstock/Getty Images; 3b: Chris Stein/Getty Images; 4tl: Thomas Marent, UK; 4tc: Papilio/Alamy; 4tr: Rosemary Clavert/Getty Images; 4bl: Comstock/Getty Images; 4bc: Global P/iStockphoto; 4br: Saje/Shutterstock; 4–5 (back): Petron Stanislav Eduardovich/Shutterstock; 5tl: Ingo Arndt/Getty Images; 5ml: Coyote Photography.co.uk/Alamy; 5mc: Pashalgnator/iStockphoto; 5bl: Fivespots/Shutterstock; 5bc: Travis Klein/Shutterstock; 5br: Darren Baker/Shutterstock; 6–7: Chris Stein/Getty Images; 7tr: Stefan1234/IStockphoto; 7m: GK Hart/Vikki Hart/Getty Images; 7bl: Maten/iStockphoto; 7bc: Saje/iStockphoto; 7br: Jim Larkin/iStockphoto; 8t: Claudia Knieling/Alamy; 8bl, 8bcl, 8bcr, 8br: Thomas Marent, UK; 9t: Comstock/Getty Images; 9bl, 9bcl, 9bcr, 9br: Thomas Marent, UK; 10: Bob Elsdale/Getty Images; 11tr: Alex Branwell/Getty Images; 11tc: Rosemary Calvert/Getty Images; 11ml: Burazin/Getty Images; 11mr, 11b: Geoff Dann/Getty Images; 12: Frans Lanting/Corbis; 13tl: Mitsuaki Iwago/Minden/Getty Images; 13tc: David Courtney/Getty Images; 13tr: Theo Allofs/Getty Images; 13b: Eric Isselee/Shutterstock; 14tr: BW Fohsom/Shutterstock; 14bl: Kim Taylor/Getty Images; 14bcl, 14bcr: Neil Fletcher/Getty Images; 14br: Dave King/DK/Getty Images; 15t: David Fleetham/Visuals Unlimited; 15b: Design Pics, Inc/Alamy; 16–17: Jean-Paul Nacivet/Getty Images; 17tl: Val/Getty Images; 17tc: Buena Vista Images/Getty Images; 17tr: Dbtale/Shutterstock; 18tr: Tischanko Irina/Shutterstock; 18ml: Lilkar/Shutterstock; 18mc: Stephen Dalton/Minden/Getty Images; 18mr: Heidi & Hans-Juergen Koch/Minden/Getty Images; 18b: Alex Wild Photography, Champaign-Urbana, IL; 18–19 (back): Tischanko Irina/Shutterstock; 19tl: Alle/Dreamstime; 19ml: Eric Tourneret/Visuals Unlimited, Inc.; 20tr: Eric Isselee/Shutterstock; 20ml: Lockwood, C.C./Animals Animals Earth Scenes; 20b: Netfalls/Shutterstock; 21tl, 21tc, 21tr: Heiko Kiera/Shutterstock; 21b: Chris Johns/National Geographic Images; 22: Martin Strmiska/Seapics; 23tra: Rion819/IStockphoto; 23trb: CBPix/iStockphoto; 23mr: Global P/iStockphoto; 23bl: Louise Murray/Alamy; 23bc: Water Frame/Alamy; 23br: Doug Perrine/Seapics; 24tr: Global P/iStockphoto; 24–25: Radius Images/Corbis; 25tl: Mari_Art/iStockphoto; 25t: PBPA Paul Beard Photo Agency/Alamy; 25ma: Einarsson, Palmi/Index Stock/Corbis; 25mb: I. Akhundova/Shutterstock; 25b: Juniors Bildarchiv/Alamy; 26tr: Eric Lam/Shutterstock; 26l: Eric Isselee/Shutterstock; 26br: Eric Lam/Shutterstock; 26–27m: Willee Cole/Shutterstock; 27tl: Eric Lam/Shutterstock; 27tr, 27mcl, 27mcr, 27mr, 27b: Willee Cole/Shutterstock; 28: Mira/Alamy; 29tr: P. Schwarz/Shutterstock; 29ml: Bruce MacQueen/Shutterstock; 29mc: Wendy Rentz/Shutterstock; 29mr, 29bl: Cheryl E. Davis/Shutterstock; 29bc, 29br: Martha Marks/Shutterstock; 30–31: Eric Lam/Shutterstock.

The credits for the images on page 2 can be found on pages 16–17 and 30–31.

Cover credits
Front t: Ingo Arndt/Foto Natura/Getty Images; ml: Comstock/Gettyimages; b (front): Gary Bell/Corbis; b (back): Rosemary Calvert/Getty Images. Back tl: Martin Ruegner/Getty Images; tc: Andia/Alamy; tr: Perennou Nuridsany/Photo Researchers, Inc.; ml: Dr Jeremy Burgess/Science Photo Library; mr: Daniel Cooper/Getty Images; b: Manaemedia I Dreamstime.com.